Purchased with Title I Funds

Illinois

ILLINOIS

A Buddy Book
by

Julie Murray

ABDO
Publishing Company

VISIT US AT

www.abdopub.com

Published by ABDO Publishing Company, 4940 Viking Drive, Edina, Minnesota 55435.

Copyright © 2006 by Abdo Consulting Group, Inc. International copyrights reserved in all countries. No part of this book may be reproduced in any form without written permission from the publisher. Buddy Books™ is a trademark and logo of ABDO Publishing Company.

Printed in the United States.

Edited by: Sarah Tieck
Contributing Editor: Michael P. Goecke
Graphic Design: Deb Coldiron, Maria Hosley
Image Research: Sarah Tieck
Photographs: Clipart.com, Corbis, Digital Vision, Getty Images, Library of Congress, One Mile Up, PhotoDisc, Photos.com

Library of Congress Cataloging-in-Publication Data

Murray, Julie, 1969-
     Illinois / Julie Murray.
          p. cm. — (The United States)
     ISBN 1-59197-672-3
          1. Illinois—Juvenile literature. I. Title.

F541.3.M87 2005
977.3—dc22

                                                                              2004046442

Table Of Contents

A Snapshot Of Illinois

When people think of Illinois, they think of farmland and prairies. This state is known for its fertile soil. It is full of lakes, rivers, prairies, hills, and valleys. Illinois also has large cities.

There are 50 states in the United States. Every state is different. Every state has an official state nickname. Illinois is sometimes called "The Land of Lincoln." This is because Abraham Lincoln lived in Springfield for many years. He was one of the most famous presidents of the United States.

Rolling prairies and farms are all across the state of Illinois.

There are cypress trees in the Horseshoe Lake Conservation Area of Illinois.

Illinois became the 21st state on December 3, 1818. Today, Illinois is the 24th-largest state in the United States. It has 56,343 square miles (145,928 sq km). It is home to 12,419,293 people.

Where Is Illinois?

There are four parts of the United States. Each part is called a region. Each region is in a different area of the country. The United States Census Bureau says the four regions are the Northeast, the South, the Midwest, and the West.

Illinois is in the Midwest region of the United States. Illinois has four seasons. These seasons are spring, summer, fall, and winter.

Four Regions of the United States of America

ALASKA

WASHINGTON

MONTANA

NORTH DAKOTA

MINNESOTA

VERMONT

MAINE

NEW HAMPSHIRE

MASSACHUSETTS

OREGON

IDAHO

WYOMING

SOUTH DAKOTA

WISCONSIN

MICHIGAN

NEW YORK

RHODE ISLAND

CONNECTICUT

NEVADA

UTAH

COLORADO

NEBRASKA

IOWA

ILLINOIS

INDIANA

OHIO

PENNSYLVANIA

NEW JERSEY

DELAWARE

Washington D.C.

MARYLAND

CALIFORNIA

KANSAS

MISSOURI

WEST VIRGINIA

VIRGINIA

KENTUCKY

NORTH CAROLINA

ARIZONA

NEW MEXICO

OKLAHOMA

ARKANSAS

TENNESSEE

SOUTH CAROLINA

MISSISSIPPI

ALABAMA

GEORGIA

TEXAS

LOUISIANA

FLORIDA

HAWAII

West	Midwest	South	Northeast

Illinois shares its borders with five other states. Iowa and Missouri are to the west. Wisconsin is to the north. Indiana is to the east. Kentucky is to the south. Lake Michigan is to the northeast.

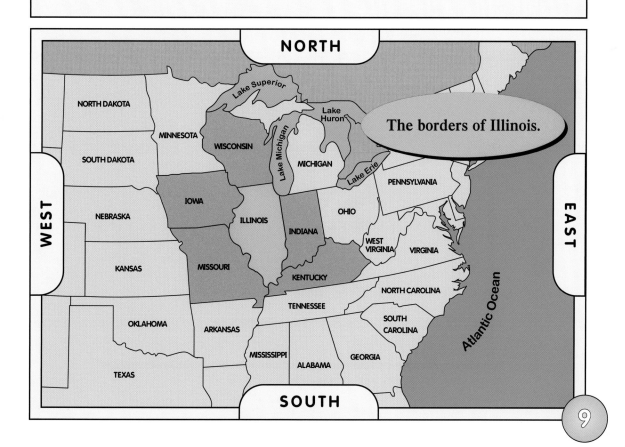

The borders of Illinois.

Illinois

State abbreviation: IL

State nickname: The Land of Lincoln

State capital: Springfield

State motto: State Sovereignty, National Union

Statehood: December 3, 1818, 21st state

Population: 12,419,293, ranks 5th

State flag:
Adopted in 1915

Land area: 56,343 square miles (145,928 sq km), ranks 24th

State tree: White Oak

State song: "Illinois"

State government: Three branches: legislative, executive, and judicial

Average July temperature: 76°F (24°C)

Average January temperature: 26°F (-3°C)

State flower:
Native violet

State animal:
White-tail deer

State bird:
Cardinal

Cities And The Capital

Chicago is the largest city in Illinois. It is the third-largest city in the United States. New York City and Los Angeles are the only cities larger than Chicago. Chicago is known as the "Windy City." Chicago sits on the banks of Lake Michigan. The lakeshore is known for its beauty.

Rockford is the second-largest city in Illinois. Aurora is the state's third-largest city. Aurora is one of many suburbs of Chicago.

The city of Chicago is on Lake Michigan.

A lighthouse on Lake Michigan

The Old State Capitol was built in 1837.

Springfield is the capital city of Illinois. It is located in the middle of the state. Abraham Lincoln lived in Springfield from 1837 to 1861. The present state capitol building was opened in 1876.

Famous Citizens

Abraham Lincoln (1809–1865)

Abraham Lincoln

Abraham Lincoln was born in Kentucky in 1809. He lived in Springfield from 1837 to 1861. Abraham Lincoln became the 16th United States president on March 4, 1861. He worked hard to end the American Civil War. Lincoln is famous for helping to end slavery, too. John Wilkes Booth shot Abraham Lincoln on April 14, 1865. This was a sad day for Americans.

Famous Citizens

Ronald Reagan (1911–2004)

Ronald Reagan was one famous person who called Illinois home. Ronald Reagan was president of the United States from 1981 to 1989. He was the 40th president of the United States. He was born in Tampico in 1911 and grew up in Dixon. People remember him for many things. Before becoming president, he was an actor in Hollywood. He was also governor of California.

Ronald Reagan

Waterways

There are many important bodies of water in Illinois.

One major waterway is the Mississippi River. The Mississippi River is one of the longest rivers in the United States. It flows 2,340 miles (3,766 km) from Minnesota to the Gulf of Mexico. It forms the entire western border of Illinois.

The first people to come to Illinois traveled the waters of the Mississippi River. Today, the Mississippi River is still a major United States river.

Many products are transported
using the Mississippi River.

Lake Michigan is one of five Great Lakes.

Another important body of water is Lake Michigan. Lake Michigan sits on the northeast border of Illinois. It is the third largest of the five Great Lakes. It is the only Great Lake that is entirely in the United States. This is why Lake Michigan is the largest body of freshwater within the borders of the United States.

The Sears Tower

The Sears Tower was completed in 1973. For more than 20 years, the Sears Tower was said to be the "World's Tallest Building." Today, it is still one of the tallest buildings in the world, and in the United States. It has 110 stories. It is 1,450 feet (442 m) tall.

The Sears Tower is in downtown Chicago.

People can see Illinois, Indiana, Wisconsin, and Michigan from the Skydeck.

More than one million people visit the Sears Tower each year. People can ride a fast elevator to the 103rd floor. A public lookout called the Skydeck is there. It takes about 70 seconds to get to the Skydeck from the ground floor.

Sports In Illinois

Chicago has many great professional sports teams. People in Illinois are known for being sports fans.

One of Chicago's teams is the Chicago Bulls. The Chicago Bulls play basketball as part of the National Basketball Association (NBA).

In the 1980s and 1990s, Michael Jordan played for the team. He is one of the greatest players to ever play basketball. The team won six championships during this time.

Michael Jordan was a famous Chicago Bulls player.

The Chicago Bears have won seven NFL titles.

The Chicago Bears are Chicago's football team. They play in the National Football League (NFL). They won the Super Bowl in 1986.

Chicago has a hockey team. It is called the Chicago Blackhawks.

The Chicago Blackhawks have won three Stanley Cups.

Chicago has two major baseball teams. One is the Chicago Cubs. The other is the Chicago White Sox.

The Chicago Cubs play in the National League. They have been playing in Chicago since 1870. The Chicago White Sox play in the American League. The White Sox are one of the original American League teams. They have been playing in Chicago since the early 1900s.

The people of Illinois can't decide whether the Chicago Cubs or the Chicago White Sox is their favorite team.

Both teams have won many pennants and awards. The two teams played against each other in the 1906 World Series. The White Sox won.

Illinois

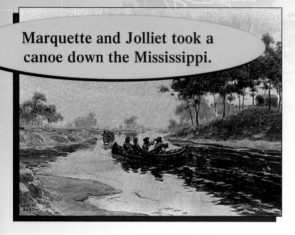

Marquette and Jolliet took a canoe down the Mississippi.

1673: Two French-Canadians explore the Mississippi and discover Illinois. They were Father Jacques Marquette and Louis Jolliet.

1818: Illinois becomes the 21st state on December 3.

1837: John Deere creates the first steel plow in Grand Detour.

1858: Stephen A. Douglas and Abraham Lincoln run for the Senate. They were famous for holding debates throughout the state of Illinois.

1860: Abraham Lincoln is elected the 16th president of the United States.

1871: A fire destroys almost every building in the city of Chicago on October 8 and 9.

The Great Chicago Fire

1909: The National Association for the Advancement of Colored People (NAACP) starts after three race riots in Illinois.

1915: Edgar Lee Masters of Chicago publishes *Spoon River Anthology*.

1942: Scientists at the University of Chicago do experiments. Their discoveries help create nuclear energy.

1950: Gwendolyn Brooks of Chicago is the first African American to win the Pulitzer Prize. She wrote a book of poems called *Annie Allen*.

1993: Many parts of Illinois are damaged by water from floods.

2005: The Abraham Lincoln Presidential Library and Museum opens in Springfield in April.

Cities in Illinois

Rockford

Grand Detour

Dixon

Chicago

Aurora

Tampico

Peoria

Bloomington

Champaign

Springfield

East St. Louis

Important Words

American Civil War the United States war between the Northern and the Southern states.

capital a city where government leaders meet.

nickname a name that describes something special about a person or a place.

nuclear a type of energy that uses atoms.

pennant a special flag that is given as a sports award.

slavery the owning of people as slaves.

Web Sites

To learn more about Illinois, visit ABDO Publishing Company on the World Wide Web. Web site links about Illinois are featured on our Book Links page. These links are routinely monitored and updated to provide the most current information available.

www.abdopub.com

Index